Copyright © 2025 by Kelly-Marie Kerr SEEK VISION

All Rights Reserved. No part of this publication may be reproduced in any form or by any means, including scanning, photocopying, or otherwise without prior written permission of the copyright holder.

UKCS Registration Number: 284447420

www.seekvision.co.uk / www.thesacredsecretion.com

ISBN 978-0685819-0-8

First Printing, 2025

Printed in the United Kingdom

DISCLAIMER:
This book contains general medical information only. NOTHING in this book is intended to be a substitute for qualified, certified professional medical or psychological advice, diagnosis, or treatment. You must NOT rely on the information in this book as an alternative to medical advice given by a professional healthcare provider or doctor. Consult a qualified professional healthcare provider or Medical Doctor (MD) with questions or concerns regarding practices or substances mentioned in this book that may affect your health or general wellbeing. You should always seek immediate professional medical attention if you think you are suffering from any medical condition. The medical information within this book is provided without any representations or warranties, express or implied. The medical information contained within this book is not professional medical advice and should not be treated as such. The medical information contained within this book is ONLY provided to highlight comparisons within the topics presented here, further personal research and professional guidance is always recommended.

ReGENEration Calendar 2026

Your **Sacred Secretion** or **Super Consciousness Awakening** practice time.

By Kelly-Marie Kerr

A tool to use alongside the *Super Consciousness Awakening Course* (available on **Teachable**).

CONTENTS

INTRODUCTION...7

WHEN THE MOON IS IN YOUR SUN SIGN...9

MACROCOSM Vs MICROCOSM..11

THE SCIENCE 13

FURTHER RESEARCH 14

THE CORRECT SACRED SECRETION TIMING 16

HOW TO READ THIS CALENDAR 18

2026 MONTHLY SACRED SECRETION CALENDAR...19

PLANNER PAGES 31

RESOURCES 104

INTRODUCTION

Your **Super Consciousness Awakening** or **Sacred Secretion practice** time is the duration of time when the moon is in your sun sign (the zodiac constellation you were born under) when observing the tropical *and* sidereal systems.

Super Consciousness Awakening is also known historically as the **Threefold Enlightenment** and esoterically as the **Great Regeneration**. More recently this inner alchemical process is referred to as the **Preservation of the Sacred Secretion.** Whatever name we choose to label it by, it is indeed *"THE GREATEST SECRET IN HUMANITY."*

From culture to culture and age to age, all throughout history, the process of awakening has been taught and known by many names. It has been described in various exoteric and esoteric ways including:

- Ignis-Aqva
- Manna from Heaven
- Merkabah Ascension
- The Alchemical Wedding
- Kundalini Rising
- 144 DNA Activation
- Clavis Rei Primae
- Xxenogenesis (nuclear fusion)
- Naronia
- The Crystalline Dew
- The Tibetan Rainbow body of Light
- The Christian Resurrection Body

Although no two understandings are identical, they each correspond with the same underlying process of super consciousness awakening.

The experience of super consciousness awakening is a true, powerful, and life-changing phenomenon that shouldn't be taken lightly, for it comes with great responsibility. Perhaps this is why there seems to have been a deliberate effort to keep our true human potential a secret.

"There is an automatic procedure within the human body, which, if not interfered with will do away with all sickness, trouble, sorrow and death, as stated in the Bible."
Page 21, God Man: The Word Made Flesh by G W Carey

"When Jesus prophesied that the Temple would be rebuilt in three days, he of course meant his own body"
Page 561, The Secret History of the World by Jonathan Black

These great minds were alluding to the inner alchemical process of **super consciousness awakening.**

Super consciousness awakening is called "threefold" because it causes changes in the body, mind and spirit. Meaning that the benefits are felt physically, mentally, and energetically.

The basis for this teaching is the understanding or "inner" standing that IN you there is a consciousness that overcomes the world. It is the "Christ" or "Super" self of you -- it is the genius or GENE-ius of you, the God-self of you that is the master within you and is the wholeness in you.

This process encourages the regeneration of every cell of your being and even activates dormant brain cells. The ancients called anyone who had this experience a "Christ" (Anointed one).

This calendar is designed to help you find the exact time of each lunar (moon) cycle, when you should do your super consciousness awakening or sacred secretion practice.

If you are looking for further guidance on what your monthly practice should include, I recommend my **"Super Consciousness Awakening"** course which is available on **Teach:able**. This course covers everything you should know about super consciousness awakening and includes several practical lessons and bonus resources to help you on your personal journey.

Alternatively, my YouTube channel "Kelly-Marie Kerr" features many practical videos, and my books contain practical guidance too.

WHEN THE MOON IS IN YOUR SUN SIGN

Italics taken from The Cell of Life: Awakening and Regenerating

There is a perpetual cycle occurring in the temple body.

The cycle causes degeneration or regeneration physically, mentally, and spiritually depending on your vibration and choices.

The regeneration of the fluidic (lunar) body happens monthly, coinciding with the moon.

The regeneration of the mineral (solar) body happens yearly, coinciding with the sun.

Each solar "year" includes 13 lunar months (there are 13 new moons per year, not 12).

Once a month, when the moon enters the zodiacal constellation that you were born under and for approximately 3.5 days thereafter, there is an opportunity for **super consciousness awakening.**

At this appointed monthly time, you receive an astral influx of stellar, planetary and lunar energy that is specific to your atomic (astral) self.

This astral influx differs for each zodiacal sign due to the atomic variables and potencies of the stars and planets in or near each constellation.

The size of the moon (crescent to full) affects the concentration of the astral influx also.

You receive your unique astral influx monthly via the Earth's satellite, the moon (which acts as a giant reflector for cosmic rays to reach you).

The reason the opportunity for **super consciousness awakening** *happens monthly is primarily due to the moons orbit reacting with the magnetite crystals in your brain.*

Stars are like nuclear reactors forging the atoms and elements that coalesce to build the molecules and cells of our body's. The composition of the astral influx changes according to stellar, planetary, and lunar positions. It is the differentiations within this energy that create the wonderful characteristics, talents, interests, and idiosyncrasies of each individual "self" (we are all made of stardust).

By mass, about 96 percent of our bodies are made of four key elements: oxygen (65 percent), carbon (18.5 percent), hydrogen (9.5 percent) and nitrogen (3.3 percent).

"When the universe started, there was just hydrogen and a little helium and very little of anything else. Stars take fuel and convert it into something else. Hydrogen is formed into helium, and helium is built into carbon, nitrogen and oxygen, iron, sulphur etc. EVERYTHING WE ARE MADE OF."
Simon Worrall, National Geographic

When the moon travels through the same position that it was in at the time of your birth, the astral influx contains the same influences, or energies that were presented to you or installed into you from or by Source (God) at the time of birth.

Your individual <u>astral influx</u> is totally bespoke and depends on your birth time, place, and day. So, when the moon traverses through your specific zodiacal sign each month, you receive an injection of life – totally custom to you!

If you follow and embody the teachings of super-conscious awakening (enlightenment) at the appointed time, this infusion of divine astral light can awaken your inner gifts, renew your spirit with vibrant life, and bring a deep clarity of who you truly are. It is a quickening energy that uplifts every part of your being—mind, body, and soul—helping you feel more alive, more aligned, and more empowered to walk your path with grace and purpose.

"When the Moon, in the course of her motion, arrives at the same point during each month, she impregnates these "seeds" and endows them with magnetic life; therefore, in an occult sense, she confers upon humanity the powers and possibilities of magical forces. It is this Luni-Solar influx of Naronia within the human constitution, then, that controls the real foundation and basis of spiritual development and occult power."
(Page 126) [Naronia] "Light of Egypt" by Thomas H. Burgoyne

MACROCOSM AND MICROCOSM
Celestial Blueprint and Lunar Activation

Knowing the in tandem processes of the outer (macro) and inner (micro) or upper (heavenly) and lower (earthly) worlds builds wisdom and understanding (gnosis), and consequently promotes favourable alchemy (chemistry) in the body.

Solar Sign (Your Birth/Zodiac Sign) -- The Star Seed
- At birth, the Sun was in a specific part of the sky – your zodiac sign. This is your solar imprint.
- Symbolically, it reflects the core of your being: your identity, spiritual "code," or "divine seed pattern."
- Esoterically, this is the starry blueprint etched into your subtle and physical body – your unique "constellation signature."

The Moon -- Waters of Activation
- The moon governs the earth's tides, our emotional body's, vital fluids, cycles, and receptivity.
- In sacred traditions, the moon represents soma, prima materia; the mother (mater/matter); and the feminine field in which life takes form.

When Moon Meets Your Sun Sign
- When the moon enters your birth/zodiac sign – it penetrates your solar code.
- This is a celestial marriage of the seed (Sun/Fire) and the womb (Moon/Water).
- It's when the blueprint reactivates – like a key entering the lock of your spiritual physiology.

Microcosm
Sun = DNA/Nucleus/Core/Pineal – Spiritual Identity
- Your nucleus (in every cell) contains your DNA, your original code.
- This is the centre of command, holding your identity in physical form.

Moon = Soma/Lymph/Cell Membrane/Pituitary – Material Identity
- The lymphatic system and extracellular fluids are highly responsive to rhythm and lunar pull.
- The cell membrane regulates what comes in and out – much like the Moon governs influence, reflection, and protection.
- Soma (in yoga/alchemy) is the nectar distilled by internal purity – mirrored by the moonlight's cool, reflective quality.

Macro (Sky)	Micro (Body)
Moon enters natal Sun sign	Moon stirs soma and the "waters" of the body touch the inner solar code
Lunar light on solar imprint/constellation	Soma nourishes your divine blueprint and DNA pattern, awakens your origin pattern (soul remembrance)
Lunar reflection of star seed	Activation of cellular memory, reorganisation and cleansing of energy and cellular terrain

Macro (Sky)	Micro (Body)
Union of solar and lunar influx	Cell birth and regeneration via union of solar (nucleus) and lunar (soma).
Cosmic rhythms and influences alter from sign-to-sign fertilising different aspects of creation	Energy is drawn from base to crown (Kundalini/sacred secretion), baptising the inner temple.
Moon completes its transit through the constellation.	The inner resurrection occurs by degree depending on our thoughts, words, emotions and actions (holistic alchemy and frequency).

In Short: The Sun is your code. The Moon is the carrier of light and water (lens and reflector). When they align in your sign, heaven and earth meet again -- in your body.

THE SCIENCE

In Quantum physics, the Implicate Order proposes that the physical, psychic, and spiritual (invisible or energetic) realms are ultimately connected. It is this connection that leaves us susceptible to various combinations of energetic stellar, planetary, and lunar influences.

The Implicate Order offers a holistic account of the human being and his environment.

The Implicate Order explains the reception of information from the environment not only via sense receptors, but also through every cell of the human organism as organic piezoelectricity.

Without the moon nothing could exist; the moon is a fundamental element of creation – a director and preserver of life itself. The moon has a significant influence on Earth. Not only does it control the salt-sea tides and influence the way in which plants and trees grow – but it influences ALL living organisms – INCLUDING US! The body's lymphatic system (including CSF) is the salty ocean of our microcosmic being and just as the moon affects tree sap and vitality, it also affects our vital fluids too!

Specialist Biodynamic Agriculture calendars, calculate the aspects of lunar and solar cycles, star constellations and the movement of planets. Such calendars are used every year by expert stock market traders, farmers, and botanists all over the world to decide when to sow, plant and harvest money, fruit, vegetables, flowers and crops. Beekeepers also utilise these types of calendars, knowing that the resonance within their hives changes at specific times as influenced by the moon.

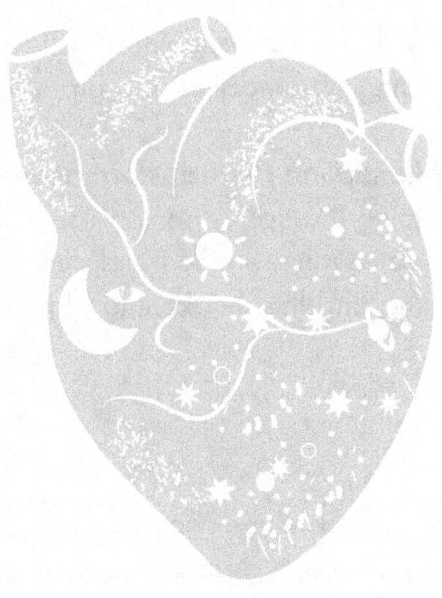

FURTHER RESEARCH

If you've purchased this calendar, the chances are that you're already primed and ready to begin your practise!

But for any sceptics or analytical minds seeking further evidence and corroboration, here are several varied sources illustrating the importance of the Moon's transits, particularly through an individual's birth or sun sign, and insightful views on how this natural rhythm can impact health, detoxification, regeneration, and spiritual growth.

The work of these beautiful and intellectual minds underscores the belief that aligning personal practices with lunar cycles can optimize physical, mental, and spiritual well-being.

CANDIDATE 1: Manly P. Hall

A renowned esoteric scholar who wrote extensively on astrology and the influence of celestial bodies on human consciousness and health. Hall believed that the Moon's phases and its transit through zodiac signs could influence both physical and spiritual well-being.

In his book **Astrological Essays,** Hall discusses how the moons transit through the zodiac, particularly when it returns to the sign it occupied at birth serves as a period of reflection and renewal, where the soul is more open to introspection, and the body to healing. He refers to it as *"a time when nature's rhythms align with the individual's inner being, offering an opportunity for regeneration."*

CANDIDATE 2: Barbara Hand Clow

An astrologer and author who discusses the Moon's influence on the body's energetic system, particularly in relation to Kundalini energy. Barbara Hand Clow believes that the Moon's transit through one's birth or sun sign can facilitate the rising of Kundalini and promote spiritual and physical healing.

In her book, **Astrology and the Rising of Kundalini: The Transformative Power of Saturn, Chiron, and Uranus** she explores how the moon traversing through a person's sun sign causes a natural amplification of energy that resonates deeply with the individual's core being and discusses how this time can be harnessed for profound healing and the awakening of latent spiritual energies, especially if one is attuned to these cycles.

CANDIDATE 3: Rudolf Steiner

Steiner, the founder of Anthroposophy, emphasized the Moon's role in influencing human health and behaviour. He believed that the Moon's cycles have a profound effect on the etheric body, which in turn influences physical and emotional health. The transit through one's birth sign was seen as a period of heightened influence.

In *The Influence of the Stars on Human Life and the Earth* – a collection of Steiner's lectures and writings on astrology he explains how the position of the Moon in relation to one's natal chart plays a significant role in the ebb and flow of life forces within the individual. Observing that the Moons alignment with the natal Sun provides a strong connection to the etheric body offering a period for potent spiritual and physical renewal.

CANDIDATE 4: Vivi Stamatatos

In *Astrological Secrets for the New Millennium*, Vivi Stamatatos discusses the Moon's transits in detail, particularly how they can be used to time health regimens and spiritual practices. She emphasizes the importance of understanding how the Moon interacts with an individual's natal chart to optimize health and personal growth.

CANDIDATE 5: Max Heindel

An esoteric Christian mystic, and astrologer who wrote about the spiritual and physical impacts of celestial bodies on humans. Heindel highlighted the Moon's transit through the birth sign as a time of increased sensitivity, making it ideal for spiritual work and physical regeneration.

In *The Message of the Stars*, Heindel explains that when the moons passage through the individual's birth sign is highly significant for the absorption of cosmic energies, which can be used to strengthen the body and elevate the soul. Describing this as a time when one's spiritual and physical faculties are most receptive.

CANDIDATE 6: Edgar Cayce

Edgar Cayce, often called the "sleeping prophet," gave readings that touched on astrology, including the Moon's influence on health and spirituality. His readings suggested that the Moon's transit through an individual's birth or sun sign can influence physical and mental health, making it a good time for introspection and healing practices.

In *Edgar Cayce's Astrology for the Soul by Margaret Gammon*, this concept is explored in detail, specifically discussing how the moon passing through the same sign as that of the individual's birth brings about certain influences that may be used for good or ill, depending on the individual's attunement.

~ ~ ~

Other interesting voices on this subject include the pioneering astrologer and psychologist Dane Rudhyar and the astrologer turned researcher and author Demetra George.

In conclusion, there are many fascinating, diverse and credible sources that emphasize the importance of moon and star alignments and the transformational potential that these relations create for our us.

THE CORRECT SACRED SECRETION TIMING

You may already know that astrology can be tracked using more than one system. The two most common systems are **tropical** and **sidereal.** Both play an important role in determining the true timing of the sacred secretion practice and here's why.

"Everything under creation is represented in the soil (earth) and in the stars (heavens). Everything has two witnesses, one on earth and one in the sky."
Page 1, The Night Sky of the Boorong by John Morieson

We can measure time by **the seasons (tropical time)** or by **the stars (sidereal time). Simply put, the tropical system is the earth-bound perspective, and the sidereal system represents the heavenly perspective.**

TROPICAL

The Tropical Zodiac is the position of the sun **referenced against the earth's horizon.**

The tropical system divides earth's 360 circular degrees into 12 equal zones of 300 degrees each (300 x 12 = 360). At the time of your birth (from an earth perspective), the sun was in one of those 12 zones, this is what determines your tropical sun/zodiac sign.

"Tropical" is derived from "tropos" (τροπή), meaning turning or change of direction. This specifically referred to the Sun's "turning back" at the solstices – when it stops moving higher or lower in the sky and reverses its apparent path.

SIDEREAL

The Sidereal Zodiac is the position of the sun **referenced against the stars.**

The word "sidereal" is derived from Latin "sidus" meaning "star." The Sidereal Zodiac uses the physical star constellations as their frame of reference for the sun, moon and planet positions in the sky.

The sun, moon and planets only traverse in front of 12 or 13 constellations (dubbed zodiac signs). Whether there are 12 or 13 depends on where the boundaries for the various constellations are positioned. Different cultures and systems have positioned and divided the stars differently. Lahiri's Sidereal (Vedic) precision astrology uses 12 as does this calendar.

TROPICAL AND SIDEREAL TOGETHER

"We are observers standing on the surface of the Earth and gazing at the sky. In our minds eye we can also visualise being outside our galaxy looking in."
A Journey towards Freedom and Love by B. Keats

In other words, we are both the earth and the stars, both perspectives (tropical and sidereal) are relative in our physical and ethereal makeup. Both systems can be compared against one another, this alignment makes one comprehensive calculator.

When represented as wheels they can be superimposed using the sun as the common point. **From this holistic view we see that the heavenly zodiac (sidereal) is imprinted into the earth (tropical zodiac).**

This is why BOTH systems are used in Biodynamic Agriculture, and why BOTH systems should be used to find your super consciousness awakening practice time.

During the tropical timing the moon glides through the outskirts of your zodiac, and during the sidereal time you will be poised for the great regeneration.

A controversial quote from Doctor Carey in the book **GOD MAN: The Word Made Flesh** says,

"These designing schemers suppressed the truth in order to stop people from realising what is meant by 'the heavens declare the glory of God.' The moon, in its monthly round of 29.5 days enters the outer stars of a constellation (tropical) 2.5 days before it enters the central stars of the constellations (sidereal) that are known as the signs of the zodiac. But to this day the whole antiChrist world go by tropical system that makes the moon enter a sign of the zodiac 2.5 days before it does enter it and thus perpetuates a lie!"

This excerpt would lead us to believe that the sidereal system is the correct one to follow and it is true that the tropical system is more or less 2.5 days "ahead" of the sidereal system. However, the difference between the two systems is a simple matter of space, distance, and perspective and both bear relevance in our temple bodies due to the hermetic law of correspondence.

In conclusion, you need to do your super consciousness awakening (sacred secretion) practice when the moon is moving through your zodiacal sign on both the tropical and sidereal calendars.

This calendar shows you your specific days at a glance. All you need to do is find the symbol for your zodiac (the sun sign you were born under) on each month and those will be the days that you should do your practice.

In summary, distant stars as well as our local Sun (which is also a star) and planets emanate an invisible astral influence (atomic energy) which alters due to the position of the moon and the energies gathered or distributed by it. This astral influx is known as "solar seeds" in occultism and the "solar wind" in modern science. Scientifically speaking, the earth's magnetosphere deflects the "solar wind" (a supersonic stream of charged particles) toward earth.

The solar wind is a plasma that consists of charged atoms, originally formed by photons. Photons are also known as "quanta," "packets of light," and "electromagnetic energy" – this light, whatever we call it is at the origin or source of life itself. Under a microscope it can be seen that photons have the form of what's known as the "seed of life" in sacred geometry. The "seed of life" is made up of seven interlocking circles also known as the "Genesis Pattern".

If you want to know more about how the light or photons convert into electrons and subsequently minerals (cell-salts) and CSF in the body, then please read **The Cell of Life: Awakening and Regenerating.**

HOW TO READ THIS CALENDAR

The top line on each day shows which sun sign (zodiac) the moon is in for the **tropical calculations.**

The second line on each day shows which sun sign (zodiac) the moon is in for the **sidereal calculations.**

I have then numbered the days to show the duration of time the moon spends in that constellation **including both systems.**

For example, a "1" represents the first day the moon is in that particular sign, a "2" refers to the second day and so on.

This year I have also included the **specific tropical start time** and **sidereal end time;** these are written in smaller text under the sign and number (some finish part way through the following day).

To find your regeneration or super consciousness awakening practice days, simply find the date that shows your sun sign coupled with the number "1." This is the day you should begin.

You should complete your practice time on the last date showing your sun sign, this will either be coupled with a "4" or a "5".

This example shows the Sacred Secretion practice time for Leo in the month of January 2026:

	SUNDAY	MONDAY	TUESDAY	WEDNESDAY	THURSDAY	FRIDAY	SATURDAY
TROPICAL		29 TAURUS 1 ♉ phase begins @ 11:57	30 TAURUS 2	31 GEMINI 1 ♊ phase begins @ 13:12	1 GEMINI 2	2 CANCER 1 ♋ phase begins @ 13:08	3 CANCER 2
SIDEREAL		ARIES 3	ARIES 4 ♈ phase ends @ 03:53 (31st)	TAURUS 3	TAURUS 4 ♉ phase ends @ 03:56 (2nd)	GEMINI 3	GEMINI 4 ♊ phase ends @ 05:40 (4th)
TROPICAL	4 LEO 1 ♌ phase begins @ 13:43	5 LEO 2	6 VIRGO 1 ♍ phase begins @ 16:56	7 VIRGO 2	8 VIRGO 3	9 LIBRA 1 ♎ phase begins @ 00:05	10 LIBRA 2
SIDEREAL	CANCER 3	CANCER 4 ♋ phase ends @ 05:57 (6th)	LEO 3	LEO 4 ♌ phase ends @ 05:56 (8th)	VIRGO 3	VIRGO 4	VIRGO 5 ♍ phase ends @ 23:23 (10th)

"The sun and moon are, to us, transmitters of stellar forces. They cast their gathered or reflected potencies into our magnetic atmosphere."

(Page 206) "The Light of Egypt" by Thomas H. Burgoyne

"The sun and moon are, to us, transmitters of stellar forces. They cast their gathered or reflected potencies into our magnetic atmosphere."

Thomas H. Burgoyne

JANUARY 2026

SUNDAY	MONDAY	TUESDAY	WEDNESDAY	THURSDAY	FRIDAY	SATURDAY
TROPICAL / **SIDEREAL**	**29** TAURUS 1 ♉ phase begins @ 11:57 **ARIES 3**	**30** TAURUS 2 **ARIES 4** ♈ phase ends @ 03:53 (31st)	**31** GEMINI 1 ♊ phase begins @ 13:12 **TAURUS 3**	**1** GEMINI 2 **TAURUS 4** ♉ phase ends @ 03:56 (2nd)	**2** CANCER 1 ♋ phase begins @ 13:08 **GEMINI 3**	**3** CANCER 2 **GEMINI 4** ♊ phase ends @ 05:40 (4th)
4 LEO 1 ♌ phase begins @ 13:43 **CANCER 3**	**5** LEO 2 **CANCER 4** ♋ phase ends @ 05:57 (6th)	**6** VIRGO 1 ♍ phase begins @ 16:56 **LEO 3**	**7** VIRGO 2 **LEO 4** ♌ phase ends @ 05:56 (8th)	**8** VIRGO 3 **VIRGO 3**	**9** LIBRA 1 ♎ phase begins @ 00:05 **VIRGO 4**	**10** LIBRA 2 **VIRGO 5** ♍ phase ends @ 23:23 (10th)
11 SCORPIO 1 ♏ phase begins @ 10:55 **LIBRA 3**	**12** SCORPIO 2 **LIBRA 4** ♎ phase ends @ 11:52 (13th)	**13** SAGITTARIUS 1 ♐ phase begins @ 23:33 **SCORPIO 3**	**14** SAGITTARIUS 2 **SCORPIO 4**	**15** SAGITTARIUS 3 **SCORPIO 5** ♏ phase ends @ 00:18 (16th)	**16** ♑ CAPRICORN 1 phase begins @ 11:46 **SAGITTARIUS 4**	**17** CAPRICORN 2 **SAGITTARIUS 5** ♐ phase ends @ 11:11 (18th)
18 AQUARIUS 1 ♒ phase begins @ 22:17 **CAPRICORN 3**	**19** AQUARIUS 2 **CAPRICORN 4**	**20** AQUARIUS 3 **CAPRICORN 5** ♑ phase ends @ 20:06 (20th)	**21** PISCES 1 ♓ phase begins @ 06:49 **AQUARIUS 4**	**22** PISCES 2 **AQUARIUS 5** ♒ phase ends @ 03:04 (23rd)	**23** ARIES 1 ♈ phase begins @ 13:25 **PISCES 3**	**24** ARIES 2 **PISCES 4** ♓ phase ends @ 02:11 (25th)
25 TAURUS 1 ♉ phase begins @ 18:05 **ARIES 3**	**26** TAURUS 2 **ARIES 4** ♈ phase ends @ 11:15 (27th)	**27** GEMINI 1 ♊ phase begins @ 20:54 **TAURUS 3**	**28** GEMINI 2 **TAURUS 4** ♉ phase ends @ 13:01 (29th)	**29** CANCER 1 ♋ phase begins @ 22:31 **GEMINI 3**	**30** CANCER 2 **GEMINI 4**	**31** CANCER 3 **GEMINI 5** ♊ phase ends @ 14:00 (31st)

INTENTION   **DOWNLOADS AND INSPIRATION**

FEBRUARY 2026

> "During this moon/star alignment the CLAUStrum in the brain receives a bespoke astral and photon-light influx; consequently, the "presents" (presence) of Santa (Spirit) visits every cell (house) of the body."
>
> Kelly-Marie Kerr (Christmas Alchemy)

SUNDAY	MONDAY	TUESDAY	WEDNESDAY	THURSDAY	FRIDAY	SATURDAY
1 LEO 1 ♌ phase begins @ 00:08 **CANCER 4**	**2** LEO 2 **CANCER 5** ♋ phase ends @ 14:08 (2nd)	**3** VIRGO 1 ♍ phase begins @ 03:20 **LEO 3**	**4** VIRGO 2 **LEO 4** ♌ phase ends @ 13:53 (4th)	**5** LIBRA 1 ♎ phase begins @ 09:32 **VIRGO 3**	**6** LIBRA 2 **VIRGO 4** ♍ phase ends @ 07:52 (7th)	**7** SCORPIO 1 ♏ phase begins @ 19:12 **LIBRA 3**
8 SCORPIO 2 **LIBRA 4**	**9** SCORPIO 3 **LIBRA 5** ♎ phase ends @ 19:42 (9th)	**10** SAGITTARIUS 1 ♐ phase begins @ 07:21 **SCORPIO 4**	**11** SAGITTARIUS 2 **SCORPIO 5** ♏ phase ends @ 08:13 (12th)	**12** CAPRICORN 1 ♑ phase begins @ 19:44 **SAGITTARIUS 3**	**13** CAPRICORN 2 **SAGITTARIUS 4**	**14** CAPRICORN 3 **SAGITTARIUS 5** ♐ phase ends @ 19:16 (14th)
15 AQUARIUS 1 ♒ phase begins @ 06:16 **CAPRICORN 4**	**16** AQUARIUS 2 **CAPRICORN 5** ♑ phase ends @ 03:36 (17th)	**17** PISCES 1 ♓ phase begins @ 14:08 **AQUARIUS 3**	**18** PISCES 2 **AQUARIUS 4** ♒ phase ends @ 09:30 (19th)	**19** ARIES 1 ♈ phase begins @ 19:38 **PISCES 3**	**20** ARIES 2 **PISCES 4** ♓ phase ends @ 13:38 (21st)	**21** TAURUS 1 ♉ phase begins @ 23:30 **ARIES 3**
22 TAURUS 2 **ARIES 4**	**23** TAURUS 3 **ARIES 5** ♈ phase ends @ 16:43 (23rd)	**24** GEMINI 1 ♊ phase begins @ 02:28 **TAURUS 4**	**25** GEMINI 2 **TAURUS 5** ♉ phase ends @ 19:25 (25th)	**26** CANCER 1 ♋ phase begins @ 05:10 **GEMINI 3**	**27** CANCER 2 **GEMINI 4** ♊ phase ends @ 20:09 (27th)	**28** LEO 1 ♌ phase begins @ 08:16 **CANCER 3**

INTENTION

DOWNLOADS AND INSPIRATION

MARCH 2026

"The moon is in fact a powerful regulator of all our physical and energetic systems. If the moon is powerful enough to regulate the tides in the oceans, why would we discount its effect on us?"

Kac Young

SUNDAY	MONDAY	TUESDAY	WEDNESDAY	THURSDAY	FRIDAY	SATURDAY
1 LEO 2 / CANCER 4 / ♋ phase ends @ 20:14 (1st)	**2** VIRGO 1 / ♍ phase begins @ 12:33 / LEO 3	**3** VIRGO 2 / LEO 4 / ♌ phase ends @ 19:47 (3rd)	**4** LIBRA 1 / ♎ phase begins @ 18:55 / VIRGO 3	**5** LIBRA 2 / VIRGO 4	**6** LIBRA 3 / VIRGO 5 / ♍ phase ends @ 16:49 (6th)	**7** SCORPIO 1 / ♏ phase begins @ 04:01 / LIBRA 4
8 SCORPIO 2 / LIBRA 5 / ♎ phase ends @ 04:00 (9th)	**9** SAGITTARIUS 1 / ♐ phase begins @ 15:36 / SCORPIO 3	**10** SAGITTARIUS 2 / SCORPIO 4	**11** SAGITTARIUS 3 / SCORPIO 5 / ♏ phase ends @ 16:31 (11th)	**12** CAPRICORN 1 / ♑ phase begins @ 04:06 / SAGITTARIUS 4	**13** CAPRICORN 2 / SAGITTARIUS 5 / ♐ phase ends @ 04:04 (14th)	**14** AQUARIUS 1 / ♒ phase begins @ 15:13 / CAPRICORN 3
15 AQUARIUS 2 / CAPRICORN 4 / ♑ phase ends @ 12:45 (16th)	**16** PISCES 1 / ♓ phase begins @ 23:15 / AQUARIUS 3	**17** PISCES 2 / AQUARIUS 4	**18** PISCES 3 / AQUARIUS 5 / ♒ phase ends @ 18:06 (18th)	**19** ARIES 1 / ♈ phase begins @ 04:02 / PISCES 4	**20** ARIES 2 / PISCES 5 / ♓ phase ends @ 20:58 (20th)	**21** TAURUS 1 / ♉ phase begins @ 06:34 / ARIES 3
22 TAURUS 2 / ARIES 4 / ♈ phase ends @ 22:44 (22nd)	**23** GEMINI 1 / ♊ phase begins @ 08:18 / TAURUS 3	**24** GEMINI 2 / TAURUS 4 / ♉ phase ends @ 00:48 (25th)	**25** CANCER 1 / ♋ phase begins @ 10:32 / GEMINI 3	**26** CANCER 2 / GEMINI 4 / ♊ phase and @ 01:11 (27th)	**27** LEO 1 / ♌ phase begins @ 14:09 / CANCER 3	**28** LEO 2 / CANCER 4 / ♋ phase ends @ 01:10 (29th)
29 VIRGO 1 / ♍ phase begins @ 20:33 / LEO 3	**30** VIRGO 2 / LEO 4 / ♌ phase ends @ 00:41 (31st)	**31** VIRGO 3 / VIRGO 3				

INTENTION

DOWNLOADS AND INSPIRATION

21

APRIL 2026

"Primitive Christians, the Essenes, fully realised and taught the great truth that Christ was a substance contained in the spinal cord."

George Washington Carey

SUNDAY	MONDAY	TUESDAY	WEDNESDAY	THURSDAY	FRIDAY	SATURDAY
		1 TROPICAL SIDEREAL	**1** LIBRA 1 ♎ phase begins @ 03:50 VIRGO 4	**2** LIBRA 2 VIRGO 5 ♍ phase ends @ 00:59 (3rd)	**3** SCORPIO 1 ♏ phase begins @ 13:10 LIBRA 3	**4** SCORPIO 2 LIBRA 4 ♎ phase ends @ 11:59 (5th)
5 SCORPIO 3 SCORPIO 3	**6** SAGITTARIUS 1 ♐ phase begins @ 00:31 SCORPIO 4	**7** SAGITTARIUS 2 SCORPIO 5 ♏ phase ends @ 00:24 (8th)	**8** CAPRICORN 1 ♑ phase begins @ 13:04 SAGITTARIUS 3	**9** CAPRICORN 2 SAGITTARIUS 4 phase ends @ 12:34 (10th)	**10** CAPRICORN 3 CAPRICORN 3	**11** AQUARIUS 1 ♒ phase begins @ 00:55 CAPRICORN 4
12 AQUARIUS 2 CAPRICORN 5 ♑ phase ends @ 22:15 (12th)	**13** PISCES 1 ♓ phase begins @ 9:55 AQUARIUS 3	**14** PISCES 2 AQUARIUS 4 ♒ phase ends @ 04:08 (15th)	**15** ARIES 1 ♈ phase begins @ 15:03 PISCES 3	**16** ARIES 2 PISCES 4 ♓ phase ends @ 06:33 (17th)	**17** TAURUS 1 ♉ phase begins @ 16:57 ARIES 3	**18** TAURUS 2 ARIES 4 ♈ phase ends @ 07:02 (19th)
19 GEMINI 1 ♊ phase begins @ 17:17 TAURUS 3	**20** GEMINI 2 TAURUS 4 ♉ phase ends @ 07:31 (21st)	**21** CANCER 1 ♋ phase begins @ 18:00 GEMINI 3	**22** CANCER 2 GEMINI 4 ♊ phase ends @ 08:16 (23rd)	**23** LEO 1 ♌ phase begins @ 20:40 CANCER 3	**24** LEO 2 CANCER 4 ♋ phase ends @ 08:09 (25th)	**25** LEO 3 LEO 3
26 VIRGO 1 ♍ phase begins @ 02:04 LEO 4 ♌ phase ends @ 07:39 (27th)	**27** VIRGO 2 VIRGO 2	**28** LIBRA 1 ♎ phase begins @ 10:02 VIRGO 3	**29** LIBRA 2 VIRGO 4 ♍ phase ends @ 07:45 (30th)	**30** SCORPIO 1 ♏ phase begins @ 20:01 LIBRA 3		

INTENTION

DOWNLOADS AND INSPIRATION

MAY 2026

> "The 3.5 coils of the kundalini "serpent", point to the 3.5 days that Jesus spent in the tomb prior to his resurrection and the time the moon spends in each sign during its cycle."
>
> Kelly-Marie Kerr (Christmas Alchemy).

SUNDAY	MONDAY	TUESDAY	WEDNESDAY	THURSDAY	FRIDAY	SATURDAY
				TROPICAL **SIDEREAL**	**1** SCORPIO 2 **LIBRA 4**	**2** SCORPIO 3 **LIBRA 5** ♎ phase ends @ 19:00 (2nd)
3 SAGITTARIUS 1 ♐ phase begins @ 7:33 **SCORPIO 4**	**4** SAGITTARIUS 2 **SCORPIO 5** ♏ phase ends @ 07:25 (5th)	**5** CAPRICORN 1 ♑ phase begins @ 20:05 **SAGITTARIUS 3**	**6** CAPRICORN 2 **SAGITTARIUS 4**	**7** CAPRICORN 3 **SAGITTARIUS 5** ♐ phase ends @ 19:57 (7th)	**8** AQUARIUS 1 ♒ phase begins @ 08:27 **CAPRICORN 4**	**9** AQUARIUS 2 **CAPRICORN 5** ♑ phase ends @ 06:43 (10th)
10 PISCES 1 ♓ phase begins @ 18:39 **AQUARIUS 3**	**11** PISCES 2 **AQUARIUS 4** ♒ phase ends @ 13:55 (12th)	**12** PISCES 3 **PISCES 3**	**13** ARIES 1 ♈ phase begins @ 01:03 **PISCES 4**	**14** ARIES 2 **PISCES 5** ♓ phase ends @ 17:04 (14th)	**15** TAURUS 1 ♉ phase begins @ 3:30 **ARIES 3**	**16** TAURUS 2 **ARIES 4** ♈ phase ends @ 17:17 (16th)
17 GEMINI 1 ♊ phase begins @ 03:22 **TAURUS 3**	**18** GEMINI 2 **TAURUS 4** ♉ phase ends @ 16:35 (18th)	**19** CANCER 1 ♋ phase begins @ 02:45 **GEMINI 3**	**20** CANCER 2 **GEMINI 4** ♊ phase ends @ 17:07 (20th)	**21** LEO 1 ♌ phase begins @ 03:47 **CANCER 3**	**22** LEO 2 **CANCER 4** ♋ phase ends @ 17:00 (22nd)	**23** VIRGO 1 ♍ phase begins @ 07:56 **LEO 3**
24 VIRGO 2 **LEO 4** ♌ phase ends @ 16:29 (24th)	**25** LIBRA 1 ♎ phase begins @ 15:33 **VIRGO 3**	**26** LIBRA 2 **VIRGO 4** ♍ phase ends @ 13:30 (27th)	**27** LIBRA 3 **LIBRA 3**	**28** SCORPIO 1 ♏ phase begins @ 01:52 **LIBRA 4**	**29** SCORPIO 2 **LIBRA 5** ♎ phase ends @ 01:09 (30th)	**30** SAGITTARIUS 1 ♐ phase begins @ 13:44 **SCORPIO 3**
31 SAGITTARIUS 2 **SCORPIO 4** ♏ phase ends @ 13:39 (1st)						

INTENTION   **DOWNLOADS AND INSPIRATION**

> "Every month in the life of every man or woman, when the moon is in the sign that the sun was in at the birth of the individual, there is a psycho-physical seed or 'Son of Man' born in the Solar Plexus or the pneumo-gastric plexus which in the ancient text was called the 'House of Bread.'"
>
> George Washington Carey

JUNE 2026

SUNDAY	MONDAY	TUESDAY	WEDNESDAY	THURSDAY	FRIDAY	SATURDAY
TROPICAL **SIDEREAL**	**1** SAGITTARIUS 3 **SAGITTARIUS 3**	**2** CAPRICORN 1 ♑ phase begins @ 02:19 **SAGITTARIUS 4**	**3** CAPRICORN 2 **SAGITTARIUS 5** ♐ phase ends @ 02:12 (4th)	**4** AQUARIUS 1 ♒ phase begins @ 14:45 **CAPRICORN 3**	**5** AQUARIUS 2 **CAPRICORN 4** ♑ phase ends @ 13:34 (6th)	**6** AQUARIUS 3 **AQUARIUS 3**
7 PISCES 1 ♓ phase begins @ 01:42 **AQUARIUS 4**	**8** PISCES 2 **AQUARIUS** ♒ phase ends @ 22:07 (8th)	**9** ARIES 1 ♈ phase begins @ 09:33 **PISCES 3**	**10** ARIES 2 **PISCES 4** ♓ phase ends @ 02:47 (11th)	**11** TAURUS 1 ♉ phase begins @ 13:27 **ARIES 3**	**12** TAURUS 2 **ARIES 4** ♈ phase ends @ 03:56 (13th)	**13** GEMINI 1 ♊ phase begins @ 14:05 **TAURUS 3**
14 GEMINI 2 **TAURUS** ♉ phase ends @ 03:11 (15th)	**15** CANCER 1 ♋ phase begins @ 13:14 **GEMINI 3**	**16** CANCER 2 **GEMINI 4** ♊ phase ends @ 03:39 (17th)	**17** LEO 1 ♌ phase begins @ 13:04 **CANCER 3**	**18** LEO 2 **CANCER 4** ♋ phase ends @ 03:35 (19th)	**19** VIRGO 1 ♍ phase begins @ 15:36 **LEO 3**	**20** VIRGO 2 **LEO 4** ♌ phase ends @ 03:09 (21st)
21 LIBRA 1 ♎ phase begins @ 21:54 **VIRGO 3**	**22** LIBRA 2 **VIRGO 4**	**23** LIBRA 3 **VIRGO 5** ♍ phase ends @ 19:23 (23rd)	**24** SCORPIO 1 ♏ phase begins @ 07:43 **LIBRA 4**	**25** SCORPIO 2 **LIBRA 5** ♎ phase ends @ 07:04 (26th)	**26** SAGITTARIUS 1 ♐ phase begins @ 19:40 **SCORPIO 3**	**27** SAGITTARIUS 2 **SCORPIO 4**
28 SAGITTARIUS 3 **SCORPIO 5** ♏ phase ends @ 19:39 (28th)	**29** CAPRICORN 1 ♑ phase begins @ 08:18 **SAGITTARIUS 4**	**30** CAPRICORN 2 **SAGITTARIUS 5** ♐ phase ends @ 08:02 (1st)				

INTENTION

DOWNLOADS AND INSPIRATION

> "The magic of Christmas is all encompassing. It happens in the dance of macrocosmic objects, like the sun and the moon in the sky (solstice), in nature, and it happens inside us."
>
> Kelly-Marie Kerr (Christmas Alchemy)

JULY 2026

SUNDAY	MONDAY	TUESDAY	WEDNESDAY	THURSDAY	FRIDAY	SATURDAY
		1 TROPICAL SIDEREAL	**1** AQUARIUS 1 phase begins @ 20:32 CAPRICORN 3	**2** AQUARIUS 2 CAPRICORN 4	**3** AQUARIUS 3 CAPRICORN 5 phase ends @ 19:19 (3rd)	**4** PISCES 1 phase begins @ 07:29 AQUARIUS 4
5 PISCES 2 AQUARIUS 5 phase ends @ 04:28 (6th)	**6** ARIES 1 phase begins @ 16:06 PISCES 3	**7** ARIES 2 PISCES 4 phase ends @ 10:31 (8th)	**8** TAURUS 1 phase begins @ 21:30 ARIES 3	**9** TAURUS 2 ARIES 4 phase ends @ 13:15 (10th)	**10** GEMINI 1 phase begins @ 23:41 TAURUS 3	**11** GEMINI 2 TAURUS 4 phase ends @ 13:37 (12th)
12 CANCER 1 phase begins @ 23:46 GEMINI 3	**13** CANCER 2 GEMINI 4 phase ends @ 13:50 (14th)	**14** LEO 1 phase begins @ 23:34 CANCER 3	**15** LEO 2 CANCER 4 phase ends @ 13:55 (16th)	**16** LEO 3 LEO 3	**17** VIRGO 1 phase begins @ 01:06 LEO 4 phase ends @ 13:47 (18th)	**18** VIRGO 2 VIRGO 2
19 LIBRA 1 phase begins @ 05:56 VIRGO 3	**20** LIBRA 2 VIRGO 4 phase ends @ 02:25 (21st)	**21** SCORPIO 1 phase begins @ 14:34 LIBRA 3	**22** SCORPIO 2 LIBRA 4 phase ends @ 13:32 (23rd)	**23** SCORPIO 3 SCORPIO 3	**24** SAGITTARIUS 1 phase begins @ 02:06 SCORPIO 4	**25** SAGITTARIUS 2 SCORPIO 5 phase ends @ 02:05 (26th)
26 CAPRICORN 1 phase begins @ 14:44 SAGITTARIUS 3	**27** CAPRICORN 2 SAGITTARIUS 4	**28** CAPRICORN 3 SAGITTARIUS 5 phase ends @ 14:20 (28th)	**29** AQUARIUS 1 phase begins @ 02:45 CAPRICORN 4	**30** AQUARIUS 2 CAPRICORN 5 phase ends @ 01:09 (31st)	**31** PISCES 1 phase begins @ 13:13 AQUARIUS 3	

INTENTION

DOWNLOADS AND INSPIRATION

"And after three days and an half, the Spirit of life from God entered into them, and they stood upon their feet"

Rev 11:11 (KJV)

AUGUST 2026

SUNDAY	MONDAY	TUESDAY	WEDNESDAY	THURSDAY	FRIDAY	SATURDAY
					TROPICAL **SIDEREAL**	1 PISCES 2 **AQUARIUS 4** ♒ phase ends @ 09:57 (2nd)
2 ARIES 1 ♈ phase begins @ 21:36 **PISCES 3**	3 ARIES 2 **PISCES 4**	4 ARIES 3 **PISCES 5** ♓ phase ends @ 16:25 (4th)	5 TAURUS 1 ♉ phase begins @ 03:35 **ARIES 4**	6 TAURUS 2 **ARIES 5** ♈ phase ends @ 20:24 (6th)	7 GEMINI 1 ♊ phase begins @ 07:07 **TAURUS 3**	8 GEMINI 2 **TAURUS 4** ♉ phase ends @ 22:19 (8th)
9 CANCER 1 ♋ phase begins @ 08:45 **GEMINI 3**	10 CANCER 2 **GEMINI 4** ♊ phase ends @ 22:35 (10th)	11 LEO 1 ♌ phase begins @ 09:37 **CANCER 3**	12 LEO 2 **CANCER 4** ♋ phase ends @ 22:48 (12th)	13 VIRGO 1 ♍ phase begins @ 11:17 **LEO 3**	14 VIRGO 2 **LEO 4** ♌ phase ends @ 22:39 (14th)	15 LIBRA 1 ♎ phase begins @ 15:19 **VIRGO 3**
16 LIBRA 2 **VIRGO 4** ♍ phase ends @ 10:50 (17th)	17 SCORPIO 1 ♏ phase begins @ 22:45 **LIBRA 3**	18 SCORPIO 2 **LIBRA 4**	19 SCORPIO 3 **LIBRA 5** ♎ phase ends @ 21:01 (19th)	20 SAGITTARIUS 1 ♐ phase begins @ 09:29 **SCORPIO 4**	21 SAGITTARIUS 2 **SCORPIO 5** ♏ phase ends @ 09:20 (22nd)	22 CAPRICORN 1 ♑ phase begins @ 21:58 **SAGITTARIUS 3**
23 CAPRICORN 2 **SAGITTARIUS 4**	24 CAPRICORN 3 **SAGITTARIUS 5** ♐ phase ends @ 21:37 (24th)	25 AQUARIUS 1 ♒ phase begins @ 10:01 **CAPRICORN 4**	26 AQUARIUS 2 **CAPRICORN 5** ♑ phase ends @ 08:06 (27th)	27 PISCES 1 ♓ phase begins @ 20:03 **AQUARIUS 3**	28 PISCES 2 **AQUARIUS 4**	29 PISCES 3 **AQUARIUS 4** ♒ phase ends @ 16:08 (29th)
30 ARIES 1 ♈ phase begins @ 03:37 **PISCES 4**	31 ARIES 2 **PISCES 5** ♓ phase ends @ 21:54 (31st)					

INTENTION

DOWNLOADS AND INSPIRATION

"You weren't born to die. You were born to harness your full atomic capabilities!"
Charles Fillmore

SEPTEMBER 2026

SUNDAY	MONDAY	TUESDAY	WEDNESDAY	THURSDAY	FRIDAY	SATURDAY
		1 TROPICAL SIDEREAL	**1** TAURUS 1 ♉ phase begins @ 09:01 **ARIES 3**	**2** TAURUS 2 **ARIES 4** ♈ phase ends @ 01:56 (3rd)	**3** GEMINI 1 ♊ phase begins @ 12:47 **TAURUS 3**	**4** GEMINI 2 **TAURUS 4** ♉ phase ends @ 04:49 (5th)	**5** CANCER 1 ♋ phase begins @ 15:30 **GEMINI 3**
6 CANCER 2 **GEMINI 4** ♊ phase ends @ 05:15 (7th)	**7** LEO 1 ♌ phase begins @ 17:49 **CANCER 3**	**8** LEO 2 **CANCER 4** ♋ phase ends @ 05:37 (9th)	**9** VIRGO 1 ♍ phase begins @ 20:34 **LEO 3**	**10** VIRGO 2 **LEO 4** ♌ phase ends @ 05:26 (11th)	**11** VIRGO 3 **VIRGO 3**	**12** LIBRA 1 ♎ phase begins @ 00:51 **VIRGO 4**
13 LIBRA 2 **VIRGO 5** ♍ phase ends @ 19:57 (13th)	**14** SCORPIO 1 ♏ phase begins @ 07:43 **LIBRA 3**	**15** SCORPIO 2 **LIBRA 4** ♎ phase ends @ 05:20 (16th)	**16** SAGITTARIUS 1 ♐ phase begins @ 17:41 **SCORPIO 3**	**17** SAGITTARIUS 2 **SCORPIO 4**	**18** SAGITTARIUS 3 **SCORPIO 5** ♏ phase ends @ 17:15 (18th)	**19** CAPRICORN 1 ♑ phase begins @ 05:54 **SAGITTARIUS 4**
20 CAPRICORN 2 **SAGITTARIUS 5** ♐ phase ends @ 05:46 (21st)	**21** AQUARIUS 1 ♒ phase begins @ 15:31 **CAPRICORN 3**	**22** AQUARIUS 2 **CAPRICORN 4**	**23** AQUARIUS 3 **CAPRICORN 5** ♑ phase ends @ 16:27 (23rd)	**24** PISCES 1 ♓ phase begins @ 04:23 **AQUARIUS 4**	**25** PISCES 2 **AQUARIUS 5** ♒ phase ends 00:04 (26th)	**26** ARIES 1 ♈ phase begins @ 11:22 **PISCES 3**
27 ARIES 2 **PISCES 4** ♓ phase ends @ 04:47 (28th)	**28** TAURUS 1 ♉ phase begins @ 15:39 **ARIES 3**	**29** TAURUS 2 **ARIES 4** ♈ phase ends @ 07:44 (30th)	**30** GEMINI 1 ♊ phase begins @ 18:25 **TAURUS 3**			

INTENTION

DOWNLOADS AND INSPIRATION

"The tides rise and fall to steady pulses, so does the sap in the plant and all that is liquid (we are 70% water). The oceans, the weather and the plants are all dancing to the beat of this 'liquid music' orchestrated by the moon."

Brian Keats

OCTOBER 2026

SUNDAY	MONDAY	TUESDAY	WEDNESDAY	THURSDAY	FRIDAY	SATURDAY
			1 TROPICAL SIDEREAL	**1** GEMINI 2 TAURUS 4 phase ends @ 10:11 (2nd)	**2** CANCER 1 phase begins @ 20:53 GEMINI 3	**3** CANCER 2 GEMINI 4 phase ends @ 10:35 (4th)
4 LEO 1 phase begins @ 16:33 CANCER 3	**5** LEO 2 CANCER 4 phase ends @ 10:58 (6th)	**6** LEO 3 LEO 3	**7** VIRGO 1 phase begins @ 03:52 LEO 4	**8** VIRGO 2 phase ends @ 10:43 (8th) VIRGO 2	**9** LIBRA 1 phase begins @ 09:10 VIRGO 3	**10** LIBRA 2 VIRGO 4 phase ends @ 04:35 (11th)
11 SCORPIO 1 phase begins @ 16:21 LIBRA 3	**12** SCORPIO 2 LIBRA 4 phase ends @ 03:43 (13th)	**13** SCORPIO 3 SCORPIO 3	**14** SAGITTARIUS 1 phase begins @ 01:59 SCORPIO 4	**15** SAGITTARIUS 2 SCORPIO 5 phase ends @ 01:18 (16th)	**16** CAPRICORN 1 phase begins @ 13:56 SAGITTARIUS 3	**17** CAPRICORN 2 SAGITTARIUS 4
18 CAPRICORN 3 SAGITTARIUS 5 phase ends @ 14:04 (18th)	**19** AQUARIUS 1 phase begins @ 02:39 CAPRICORN 4	**20** AQUARIUS 2 CAPRICORN 5 phase ends @ 01:31 (21st)	**21** PISCES 1 phase begins @ 13:34 AQUARIUS 3	**22** PISCES 2 AQUARIUS 4 phase ends @ 09:34 (23rd)	**23** ARIES 1 phase begins @ 20:53 PISCES 3	**24** ARIES 2 PISCES 4 phase ends @ 13:52 (25th)
25 TAURUS 1 phase begins @ 23:34 ARIES 3	**26** TAURUS 2 ARIES 4	**27** TAURUS 3 ARIES 5 phase ends @ 15:37 (27th)	**28** GEMINI 1 phase begins @ 01:01 TAURUS 4 phase ends @ 13:28 (29th)	**29** GEMINI 2 GEMINI 2	**30** CANCER 1 phase begins @ 02:05 GEMINI 3 phase ends @ 13:54 (31st)	**31** CANCER 2 CANCER 2

INTENTION

DOWNLOADS AND INSPIRATION

NOVEMBER 2026

> "The pituitary is the moon of the microcosm, and its oxytocin and vasopressin secretions stimulate pineal activity i.e., melatonin "upgrades.""
>
> Kelly-Marie Kerr (Christmas Alchemy)

SUNDAY	MONDAY	TUESDAY	WEDNESDAY	THURSDAY	FRIDAY	SATURDAY
1 LEO 1 ♌ phase begins @ 04:17 **CANCER 3**	**2** LEO 2 **CANCER 4** ♋ phase ends @ 14:13 (2nd)	**3** VIRGO 1 ♍ phase begins @ 08:27 **LEO 3**	**4** VIRGO 2 **LEO 4** ♌ phase ends @ 13:45 (4th)	**5** LIBRA 1 ♎ phase begins @ 14:38 **VIRGO 3**	**6** LIBRA 2 **VIRGO 4** ♍ phase ends 11:46 (7th)	**7** SCORPIO 1 ♏ phase begins @ 22:39 **LIBRA 3**
8 SCORPIO 2 **LIBRA 4**	**9** SCORPIO 3 **LIBRA 5** ♎ phase ends @ 21:19 (9th)	**10** SAGITTARIUS 1 ♐ phase begins @ 08:35 **SCORPIO 4**	**11** SAGITTARIUS 2 **SCORPIO 5** ♏ phase ends @ 08:50 (12th)	**12** CAPRICORN 1 ♑ phase begins @ 20:27 **SAGITTARIUS 3**	**13** CAPRICORN 2 **SAGITTARIUS 4**	**14** CAPRICORN 3 **SAGITTARIUS 5** ♐ phase ends @ 21:42 (14th)
15 AQUARIUS 1 ♒ phase begins @ 09:23 **CAPRICORN 4**	**16** AQUARIUS 2 **CAPRICORN 5** ♑ phase ends @ 10:01 (17th)	**17** PISCES 1 ♓ phase begins @ 21:19 **AQUARIUS 3**	**18** PISCES 2 **AQUARIUS 4**	**19** PISCES 3 **AQUARIUS 5** ♒ phase ends @ 19:20 (19th)	**20** ARIES 1 ♈ phase begins @ 05:51 **PISCES 4**	**21** ARIES 2 **PISCES 5** ♓ phase ends @ 00:25 (22nd)
22 TAURUS 1 ♉ phase begins @ 10:09 **ARIES 3**	**23** TAURUS 2 **ARIES 4** ♈ phase ends @ 01:55 (24th)	**24** GEMINI 1 ♊ phase begins @ 11:09 **TAURUS 3**	**25** GEMINI 2 **TAURUS 4** ♉ phase ends @ 01:41 (26th)	**26** CANCER 1 ♋ phase begins @ 10:50 **GEMINI 3**	**27** CANCER 2 **GEMINI 4** ♊ phase ends @ 02:00 (28th)	**28** LEO 1 ♌ phase begins @ 11:20 **CANCER 3**
29 LEO 2 **CANCER** ♋ phase ends @ 02:14 (30th)	**30** VIRGO 1 ♍ phase begins @ 14:12 **LEO 3**					

INTENTION

DOWNLOADS AND INSPIRATION

> "Prepare the way, for I come to you with a new body and a new mind; with a casket of precious ointment and a chalice from the moon."
>
> M (Dayspring of Youth)

DECEMBER 2026

SUNDAY	MONDAY	TUESDAY	WEDNESDAY	THURSDAY	FRIDAY	SATURDAY
	TROPICAL **SIDEREAL**	**1** VIRGO 2 **LEO 4** ♌ phase ends @ 01:45 (2nd)	**2** LIBRA 1 ♎ phase begins @ 20:03 **VIRGO 3**	**3** LIBRA 2 **VIRGO 4**	**4** LIBRA 3 **VIRGO 5** ♍ phase ends @ 17:33	**5** SCORPIO 1 ♏ phase begins @ 04:34 **LIBRA 4**
6 SCORPIO 2 **LIBRA 5** ♎ phase ends @ 03:44 (7th)	**7** SAGITTARIUS 1 ♐ phase begins @ 15:06 **SCORPIO 3**	**8** SAGITTARIUS 2 **SCORPIO 4**	**9** SAGITTARIUS 3 **SCORPIO 5** ♏ phase ends @ 15:31 (9th)	**10** CAPRICORN 1 ♑ phase begins @ 03:08 **SAGITTARIUS 4**	**11** CAPRICORN 2 **SAGITTARIUS 5** ♐ phase ends @ 04:22 (12th)	**12** AQUARIUS 1 ♒ phase begins @ 16:05 **CAPRICORN 3**
13 AQUARIUS 2 **CAPRICORN 4**	**14** AQUARIUS 3 **CAPRICORN 5** ♑ phase ends @ 17:06 (14th)	**15** PISCES 1 ♓ phase begins @ 11:33 **AQUARIUS 4**	**16** PISCES 2 **AQUARIUS 5** ♒ phase ends @ 03:44 (17th)	**17** ARIES 1 ♈ phase begins @ 14:34 **PISCES 3**	**18** ARIES 2 **PISCES 4** ♓ phase ends @ 10:28 (19th)	**19** TAURUS 1 ♉ phase begins @ 20:29 **ARIES 3**
20 TAURUS 2 **ARIES 4** ♈ phase ends @ 13:06 (21st)	**21** GEMINI 1 ♊ phase begins @ 22:26 **TAURUS 3**	**22** GEMINI 2 **TAURUS 4** ♉ phase ends @ 12:56 (23rd)	**23** CANCER 1 ♋ phase begins @ 21:58 **GEMINI 3**	**24** CANCER 2 **GEMINI 4** ♊ phase ends @ 12:58 (25th)	**25** LEO 1 ♌ phase begins @ 21:12 **CANCER 3**	**26** LEO 2 **CANCER 4** ♋ phase ends @ 13:04 (27th)
27 VIRGO 1 ♍ phase begins @ 22:12 **LEO 3**	**28** VIRGO 2 **LEO 4** ♌ phase ends @ 13:02 (29th)	**29** VIRGO 3 **VIRGO 3**	**30** LIBRA 1 ♎ phase begins @ 02:26 **VIRGO 4**	**31** LIBRA 2 **VIRGO 5** ♍ phase ends @ 23:17 (31st)		

INTENTION

DOWNLOADS AND INSPIRATION

PLANNER PAGES

Use these planning pages to set your intentions and decide what practices you are going to do during your Sacred Secretion days. I'm sure you'll have your own ideas of what yoga, breathwork, prayers, exercises, or fasting practices you'd like to do, so this first table is just an example to get you started. There are many practical resources on the "Kelly-Marie Kerr" YouTube Channel, for example recipes, hemi-sync meditations, yoga sessions and CSF breath exercises. **Remember to let True Source Love be your guide, authenticity is key - so go within and ask the Holy Spirit to reveal itself and to make the perfect adjustments for you personally!**

EXAMPLE SACRED SECRETION DAY

DAY 1	
INTENTION	Hold a calm, fluid, and gracious attitude to optimise frequency, alchemy and receptivity.
REMINDERS	Drink plenty of Infused Water or other good quality water throughout the day. (infused water recipe on YouTube: Kelly-Marie Kerr). Take deep breaths and realign to calmness regularly. Don't sweat the small things, True Source Love always works everything out for my highest good.
MORNING PRACTICE	Gratitude affirmations, Yoga or Guided CSF Meditation (YouTube: Kelly-Marie Kerr).
BREAKFAST	Banana Onion Smoothie (smoothie recipes on YouTube: Kelly-Marie Kerr).
MIDDAY PRACTICE	Mantra Meditation **Example: "Miracle Mantra" or "Floods of Living Healing Energy"** (Mantras and songs available on YouTube: Kelly-Marie Kerr, Spotify and other Music Apps).
LUNCH	Nitric Oxide Booster smoothie or a delicious salad. **Maybe both depending on your own needs.** (Smoothie recipes on YouTube: Kelly-Marie Kerr).
AFTERNOON REMINDER	Take 5 deep breaths, see yourself in an impenetrable force-field of white light, think about the intentions you set for the day and feel deeply into awe and gratitude for the infinite power of True Source Love.
DINNER	Vegetable Soup with Ezekiel Bread.
EVENING PRACTICE	Nature walk, salt bath, reading inspired writings or sacred texts, Yoga, silent meditation and or prayer time. Don't overwhelm yourself by trying to do all of these things, just choose one or two and keep your mood easy and light – this way your alchemy is free to adjust and upgrade without interferences.
BEDTIME	Fall asleep thinking about all the things you are grateful for, or sending well wishes to the world.

January - Day 1

INTENTION	
REMINDERS	
MORNING PRACTICE	
BREAKFAST	
MIDDAY PRACTICE	
LUNCH	
AFTERNOON REMINDER	
DINNER	
EVENING PRACTICE	
BEDTIME	

January - Day 2

INTENTION	
REMINDERS	
MORNING PRACTICE	
BREAKFAST	
MIDDAY PRACTICE	
LUNCH	
AFTERNOON REMINDER	
DINNER	
EVENING PRACTICE	
BEDTIME	

January - Day 3

INTENTION	
REMINDERS	
MORNING PRACTICE	
BREAKFAST	
MIDDAY PRACTICE	
LUNCH	
AFTERNOON REMINDER	
DINNER	
EVENING PRACTICE	
BEDTIME	

January - Day 4

INTENTION	
REMINDERS	
MORNING PRACTICE	
BREAKFAST	
MIDDAY PRACTICE	
LUNCH	
AFTERNOON REMINDER	
DINNER	
EVENING PRACTICE	
BEDTIME	

January - Day 5

INTENTION	
REMINDERS	
MORNING PRACTICE	
BREAKFAST	
MIDDAY PRACTICE	
LUNCH	
AFTERNOON REMINDER	
DINNER	
EVENING PRACTICE	
BEDTIME	

January Journal

Write about your dreams, visions, synchronicities, feelings, and mystic experiences here.

For example, what have your practice days taught you? Did you feel any tingling sensations, or see any lights and colours? Do you feel clearer? Did you wake up with more energy? Did you experience detox symptoms? Are you excited about continuing your cleanse throughout the month and treating your temple body with loving care? Did your cravings reduce? Did you overcome any temptations or urges? Where can you dive deeper or commit further? What have you accepted, released or forgiven? Are you treating yourself the way you deserve to be treated? Is the self-care in full flow? Use this section to really download and release all of your thoughts, worries, revelations, and ponderings.

February - Day 1

INTENTION	
REMINDERS	
MORNING PRACTICE	
BREAKFAST	
MIDDAY PRACTICE	
LUNCH	
AFTERNOON REMINDER	
DINNER	
EVENING PRACTICE	
BEDTIME	

February - Day 2

INTENTION	
REMINDERS	
MORNING PRACTICE	
BREAKFAST	
MIDDAY PRACTICE	
LUNCH	
AFTERNOON REMINDER	
DINNER	
EVENING PRACTICE	
BEDTIME	

February - Day 3

INTENTION	
REMINDERS	
MORNING PRACTICE	
BREAKFAST	
MIDDAY PRACTICE	
LUNCH	
AFTERNOON REMINDER	
DINNER	
EVENING PRACTICE	
BEDTIME	

February - Day 4

INTENTION	
REMINDERS	
MORNING PRACTICE	
BREAKFAST	
MIDDAY PRACTICE	
LUNCH	
AFTERNOON REMINDER	
DINNER	
EVENING PRACTICE	
BEDTIME	

February - Day 5

INTENTION	
REMINDERS	
MORNING PRACTICE	
BREAKFAST	
MIDDAY PRACTICE	
LUNCH	
AFTERNOON REMINDER	
DINNER	
EVENING PRACTICE	
BEDTIME	

February Journal

March - Day 1

INTENTION	
REMINDERS	
MORNING PRACTICE	
BREAKFAST	
MIDDAY PRACTICE	
LUNCH	
AFTERNOON REMINDER	
DINNER	
EVENING PRACTICE	
BEDTIME	

March - Day 2

INTENTION	
REMINDERS	
MORNING PRACTICE	
BREAKFAST	
MIDDAY PRACTICE	
LUNCH	
AFTERNOON REMINDER	
DINNER	
EVENING PRACTICE	
BEDTIME	

March - Day 3

INTENTION	
REMINDERS	
MORNING PRACTICE	
BREAKFAST	
MIDDAY PRACTICE	
LUNCH	
AFTERNOON REMINDER	
DINNER	
EVENING PRACTICE	
BEDTIME	

March - Day 4

INTENTION	
REMINDERS	
MORNING PRACTICE	
BREAKFAST	
MIDDAY PRACTICE	
LUNCH	
AFTERNOON REMINDER	
DINNER	
EVENING PRACTICE	
BEDTIME	

March - Day 5

INTENTION	
REMINDERS	
MORNING PRACTICE	
BREAKFAST	
MIDDAY PRACTICE	
LUNCH	
AFTERNOON REMINDER	
DINNER	
EVENING PRACTICE	
BEDTIME	

March Journal

April - Day 1

INTENTION	
REMINDERS	
MORNING PRACTICE	
BREAKFAST	
MIDDAY PRACTICE	
LUNCH	
AFTERNOON REMINDER	
DINNER	
EVENING PRACTICE	
BEDTIME	

April - Day 2

INTENTION	
REMINDERS	
MORNING PRACTICE	
BREAKFAST	
MIDDAY PRACTICE	
LUNCH	
AFTERNOON REMINDER	
DINNER	
EVENING PRACTICE	
BEDTIME	

April - Day 3

INTENTION	
REMINDERS	
MORNING PRACTICE	
BREAKFAST	
MIDDAY PRACTICE	
LUNCH	
AFTERNOON REMINDER	
DINNER	
EVENING PRACTICE	
BEDTIME	

April - Day 4

INTENTION	
REMINDERS	
MORNING PRACTICE	
BREAKFAST	
MIDDAY PRACTICE	
LUNCH	
AFTERNOON REMINDER	
DINNER	
EVENING PRACTICE	
BEDTIME	

April - Day 5

INTENTION	
REMINDERS	
MORNING PRACTICE	
BREAKFAST	
MIDDAY PRACTICE	
LUNCH	
AFTERNOON REMINDER	
DINNER	
EVENING PRACTICE	
BEDTIME	

April Journal

May - Day 1

INTENTION	
REMINDERS	
MORNING PRACTICE	
BREAKFAST	
MIDDAY PRACTICE	
LUNCH	
AFTERNOON REMINDER	
DINNER	
EVENING PRACTICE	
BEDTIME	

May - Day 2

INTENTION	
REMINDERS	
MORNING PRACTICE	
BREAKFAST	
MIDDAY PRACTICE	
LUNCH	
AFTERNOON REMINDER	
DINNER	
EVENING PRACTICE	
BEDTIME	

May - Day 3

INTENTION	
REMINDERS	
MORNING PRACTICE	
BREAKFAST	
MIDDAY PRACTICE	
LUNCH	
AFTERNOON REMINDER	
DINNER	
EVENING PRACTICE	
BEDTIME	

May - Day 4

INTENTION	
REMINDERS	
MORNING PRACTICE	
BREAKFAST	
MIDDAY PRACTICE	
LUNCH	
AFTERNOON REMINDER	
DINNER	
EVENING PRACTICE	
BEDTIME	

May - Day 5

INTENTION	
REMINDERS	
MORNING PRACTICE	
BREAKFAST	
MIDDAY PRACTICE	
LUNCH	
AFTERNOON REMINDER	
DINNER	
EVENING PRACTICE	
BEDTIME	

May Journal

June - Day 1

INTENTION	
REMINDERS	
MORNING PRACTICE	
BREAKFAST	
MIDDAY PRACTICE	
LUNCH	
AFTERNOON REMINDER	
DINNER	
EVENING PRACTICE	
BEDTIME	

June - Day 2

INTENTION	
REMINDERS	
MORNING PRACTICE	
BREAKFAST	
MIDDAY PRACTICE	
LUNCH	
AFTERNOON REMINDER	
DINNER	
EVENING PRACTICE	
BEDTIME	

June - Day 3

INTENTION	
REMINDERS	
MORNING PRACTICE	
BREAKFAST	
MIDDAY PRACTICE	
LUNCH	
AFTERNOON REMINDER	
DINNER	
EVENING PRACTICE	
BEDTIME	

June - Day 4

INTENTION	
REMINDERS	
MORNING PRACTICE	
BREAKFAST	
MIDDAY PRACTICE	
LUNCH	
AFTERNOON REMINDER	
DINNER	
EVENING PRACTICE	
BEDTIME	

June - Day 5

INTENTION	
REMINDERS	
MORNING PRACTICE	
BREAKFAST	
MIDDAY PRACTICE	
LUNCH	
AFTERNOON REMINDER	
DINNER	
EVENING PRACTICE	
BEDTIME	

June Journal

July - Day 1

INTENTION	
REMINDERS	
MORNING PRACTICE	
BREAKFAST	
MIDDAY PRACTICE	
LUNCH	
AFTERNOON REMINDER	
DINNER	
EVENING PRACTICE	
BEDTIME	

July - Day 2

INTENTION	
REMINDERS	
MORNING PRACTICE	
BREAKFAST	
MIDDAY PRACTICE	
LUNCH	
AFTERNOON REMINDER	
DINNER	
EVENING PRACTICE	
BEDTIME	

July - Day 3

INTENTION	
REMINDERS	
MORNING PRACTICE	
BREAKFAST	
MIDDAY PRACTICE	
LUNCH	
AFTERNOON REMINDER	
DINNER	
EVENING PRACTICE	
BEDTIME	

July - Day 4

INTENTION	
REMINDERS	
MORNING PRACTICE	
BREAKFAST	
MIDDAY PRACTICE	
LUNCH	
AFTERNOON REMINDER	
DINNER	
EVENING PRACTICE	
BEDTIME	

July - Day 5

INTENTION	
REMINDERS	
MORNING PRACTICE	
BREAKFAST	
MIDDAY PRACTICE	
LUNCH	
AFTERNOON REMINDER	
DINNER	
EVENING PRACTICE	
BEDTIME	

July Journal

August - Day 1

INTENTION	
REMINDERS	
MORNING PRACTICE	
BREAKFAST	
MIDDAY PRACTICE	
LUNCH	
AFTERNOON REMINDER	
DINNER	
EVENING PRACTICE	
BEDTIME	

August - Day 2

INTENTION	
REMINDERS	
MORNING PRACTICE	
BREAKFAST	
MIDDAY PRACTICE	
LUNCH	
AFTERNOON REMINDER	
DINNER	
EVENING PRACTICE	
BEDTIME	

August - Day 3

INTENTION	
REMINDERS	
MORNING PRACTICE	
BREAKFAST	
MIDDAY PRACTICE	
LUNCH	
AFTERNOON REMINDER	
DINNER	
EVENING PRACTICE	
BEDTIME	

August - Day 4

INTENTION	
REMINDERS	
MORNING PRACTICE	
BREAKFAST	
MIDDAY PRACTICE	
LUNCH	
AFTERNOON REMINDER	
DINNER	
EVENING PRACTICE	
BEDTIME	

August - Day 5

INTENTION	
REMINDERS	
MORNING PRACTICE	
BREAKFAST	
MIDDAY PRACTICE	
LUNCH	
AFTERNOON REMINDER	
DINNER	
EVENING PRACTICE	
BEDTIME	

August Journal

September - Day 1

INTENTION	
REMINDERS	
MORNING PRACTICE	
BREAKFAST	
MIDDAY PRACTICE	
LUNCH	
AFTERNOON REMINDER	
DINNER	
EVENING PRACTICE	
BEDTIME	

September - Day 2

INTENTION	
REMINDERS	
MORNING PRACTICE	
BREAKFAST	
MIDDAY PRACTICE	
LUNCH	
AFTERNOON REMINDER	
DINNER	
EVENING PRACTICE	
BEDTIME	

September - Day 3

INTENTION	
REMINDERS	
MORNING PRACTICE	
BREAKFAST	
MIDDAY PRACTICE	
LUNCH	
AFTERNOON REMINDER	
DINNER	
EVENING PRACTICE	
BEDTIME	

September - Day 4

INTENTION	
REMINDERS	
MORNING PRACTICE	
BREAKFAST	
MIDDAY PRACTICE	
LUNCH	
AFTERNOON REMINDER	
DINNER	
EVENING PRACTICE	
BEDTIME	

September - Day 5

INTENTION	
REMINDERS	
MORNING PRACTICE	
BREAKFAST	
MIDDAY PRACTICE	
LUNCH	
AFTERNOON REMINDER	
DINNER	
EVENING PRACTICE	
BEDTIME	

September Journal

October - Day 1

INTENTION	
REMINDERS	
MORNING PRACTICE	
BREAKFAST	
MIDDAY PRACTICE	
LUNCH	
AFTERNOON REMINDER	
DINNER	
EVENING PRACTICE	
BEDTIME	

October - Day 2

INTENTION	
REMINDERS	
MORNING PRACTICE	
BREAKFAST	
MIDDAY PRACTICE	
LUNCH	
AFTERNOON REMINDER	
DINNER	
EVENING PRACTICE	
BEDTIME	

October - Day 3

INTENTION	
REMINDERS	
MORNING PRACTICE	
BREAKFAST	
MIDDAY PRACTICE	
LUNCH	
AFTERNOON REMINDER	
DINNER	
EVENING PRACTICE	
BEDTIME	

October - Day 4

INTENTION	
REMINDERS	
MORNING PRACTICE	
BREAKFAST	
MIDDAY PRACTICE	
LUNCH	
AFTERNOON REMINDER	
DINNER	
EVENING PRACTICE	
BEDTIME	

October - Day 5

INTENTION	
REMINDERS	
MORNING PRACTICE	
BREAKFAST	
MIDDAY PRACTICE	
LUNCH	
AFTERNOON REMINDER	
DINNER	
EVENING PRACTICE	
BEDTIME	

October Journal

November - Day 1

INTENTION	
REMINDERS	
MORNING PRACTICE	
BREAKFAST	
MIDDAY PRACTICE	
LUNCH	
AFTERNOON REMINDER	
DINNER	
EVENING PRACTICE	
BEDTIME	

November - Day 2

INTENTION	
REMINDERS	
MORNING PRACTICE	
BREAKFAST	
MIDDAY PRACTICE	
LUNCH	
AFTERNOON REMINDER	
DINNER	
EVENING PRACTICE	
BEDTIME	

November - Day 3

INTENTION	
REMINDERS	
MORNING PRACTICE	
BREAKFAST	
MIDDAY PRACTICE	
LUNCH	
AFTERNOON REMINDER	
DINNER	
EVENING PRACTICE	
BEDTIME	

November - Day 4

INTENTION	
REMINDERS	
MORNING PRACTICE	
BREAKFAST	
MIDDAY PRACTICE	
LUNCH	
AFTERNOON REMINDER	
DINNER	
EVENING PRACTICE	
BEDTIME	

November - Day 5

INTENTION	
REMINDERS	
MORNING PRACTICE	
BREAKFAST	
MIDDAY PRACTICE	
LUNCH	
AFTERNOON REMINDER	
DINNER	
EVENING PRACTICE	
BEDTIME	

November Journal

December - Day 1

INTENTION	
REMINDERS	
MORNING PRACTICE	
BREAKFAST	
MIDDAY PRACTICE	
LUNCH	
AFTERNOON REMINDER	
DINNER	
EVENING PRACTICE	
BEDTIME	

December - Day 2

INTENTION	
REMINDERS	
MORNING PRACTICE	
BREAKFAST	
MIDDAY PRACTICE	
LUNCH	
AFTERNOON REMINDER	
DINNER	
EVENING PRACTICE	
BEDTIME	

December - Day 3

INTENTION	
REMINDERS	
MORNING PRACTICE	
BREAKFAST	
MIDDAY PRACTICE	
LUNCH	
AFTERNOON REMINDER	
DINNER	
EVENING PRACTICE	
BEDTIME	

December - Day 4

INTENTION	
REMINDERS	
MORNING PRACTICE	
BREAKFAST	
MIDDAY PRACTICE	
LUNCH	
AFTERNOON REMINDER	
DINNER	
EVENING PRACTICE	
BEDTIME	

December - Day 5

INTENTION	
REMINDERS	
MORNING PRACTICE	
BREAKFAST	
MIDDAY PRACTICE	
LUNCH	
AFTERNOON REMINDER	
DINNER	
EVENING PRACTICE	
BEDTIME	

December Journal

Resources
Books and platforms created by the author Kelly-Marie Kerr

BOOKS:

- **Christmas Magic -- The Cosmic Story**
An illustrated designed to introduce the true meaning of Christmas to children.

- **Christmas Alchemy -- Harnessing Cosmic Energy Within**
An exploration of the deeper meaning of Christmas, both in the cosmos and in the body. Including an A-Z of secret Christmas symbols.

- **The Sacred Secretion -- Your Complete Guide to Kundalini Energy, Christ Oil, Alchemy, and the Monthly Seed.**
Kelly-Marie's latest book is a compendium of all the most important Sacred Secretion information. Including a full anatomical breakdown of the alchemical process and practical instructions to complete your own practice.

- **The God Design -- Secrets of the Body, Mind and Soul**
A thorough study and explanation of both the spiritual and physical elements that form the phenomena known as the sacred secretion. Including the full details of the biochemicals of enlightenment.

- **Elevation -- The Divine Power of the Human Body (A Study of the Bible Book of Revelation)**
The Bible book of Revelation explains the true science of enlightenment: body, mind, and soul in a dramatic, fantastical, and epic parable only 22 chapters. Elevation debunks the symbols and myths providing truth and clarity to its reader.

- **The Cell of Life -- Awakening and Regenerating**
A full disclosure of the 3-Fold Enlightenment or Great Regeneration, revealing the scientific parallel of the "Jesus" seed born in the body every lunar month. The "seed" is our opportunity for TOTAL renewal and regeneration.
"Every 29.5 days a seed is born in, or out of the solar plexus – the oil unites with the mineral salts and thus produces the monthly seed which goes into the vagus."
Page 90, GOD MAN: The Word Made Flesh by G W Carey

- **ReGENEration Calendar -- Your Super Consciousness Awakening or Sacred Secretion Times**
A full year calendar providing the sidereal and tropical dates for the moon entering each star sign (zodiac), plus guidelines and ideas to help you on your journey.

PLATFORMS:
- YouTube channel, "Kelly-Marie Kerr"
- Website, www.seekvision.co.uk / www.thesacredsecretion.com
- TikTok, @seekvision
- Instagram, @seekvision
- Facebook, @seekvision33
- Patreon, Seek Vision (Kelly-Marie Kerr) - Patreon membership includes 1 to 1 session

FREEDOM YOGA:
- Paid membership to the "Kelly-Marie Kerr" YouTube channel gives you access to 33 Essene based yoga videos that you can use to create your own playlists of any length and focus. You can then use your playlist as a custom yoga practice. **There are many other Essene Yoga sessions and Alchemy Classes in the members only section of YouTube also.**

COURSE:
- **Super consciousness Awakening**
Available on Teachable

www.ingramcontent.com/pod-product-compliance
Lightning Source LLC
Chambersburg PA
CBHW051353070526
44584CB00025B/3751